FATHER JUNIPERO SERRA

the

TRAVELING MISSIONARY

by Linda Lyngheim

illustrated by
Phyllis Garber

Langtry Publications
Van Nuys, California

To Brian

Library of Congress Catalog No. 85-082131
ISBN: 0-915369-01-X

LANGTRY PUBLICATIONS
7838 Burnet Avenue
Van Nuys, CA 91405-1051

1 2 3 4 5 6 7 8 9 10

PREFACE

California has a colorful past. Father Junipero Serra is part of it. He came from Spain to Mexico and California to teach the Indians about Christianity. He was a small man with big ideas. He founded nine missions along the coast of California.

There are no books written for children on Father Serra currently in print at the time of this publication. As a former children's librarian and author of *The Indians and the California Missions*, I decided a book needed to be written.

For three years, I researched the mission book. During this time, I became fascinated with Father Junipero Serra.

I hope this book will help fill the need for biographical information on Father Serra for elementary school children. Any quotes used in this book are factual, taken from letters or diaries.

CONTENTS

Preface 3
Birth 6
Childhood 8
School at Palma 12
Becoming a Priest 14
Dream to Become a Missionary 15
The Ship to Malaga 17
Sailing to the New World 19
By Foot to Mexico City 21
Father Serra In Mexico City 23
Adventures in Sierra Gorda 24
Wandering Preacher 27
Takeover Of Lower California Missions 28
The Trail To California 29
Founding Mission San Diego 35
Establishing a Pueblo and a Mission 39
San Antonio de Padua Mission 42
San Gabriel de Arcangel Mission 44
San Luis Obispo de Tolosa Mission 47
Trouble for the Missions 49
San Francisco de Asis Mission 50
San Juan Capistrano Mission 52
Santa Clara de Asis Mission 54
San Buenaventura Mission 56
The End of His Travels 58
Map of California Missions 59
Bibliography 61
Index 62-63

Father Junipero Serra the Traveling Missionary

BIRTH

The day began with great excitement. Cries of a newborn baby could be heard in the Serra house. Margarita happily cradled her baby in her arms. Her husband, Antonio, hammered a laurel branch on the door of their house. This custom announced to the neighbors that a son was born to the proud parents.

Later that day family and friends formed a procession. They carried the baby through the streets to the church. The priest was waiting to baptize the child. Several hours old, the baby named Miguel Jose first entered the church. The day was November 24, 1713.

Many years from that day, the child would grow up to become a priest. He would take the name of Father Junipero Serra. He would travel thousands of miles to a place we now call Mexico. And many more as a missionary founding missions in California. He would endure hardships to teach the native Indians Christianity. All this he would do for the love of God.

CHILDHOOD

Miguel Jose grew up in the town of Petra on the island of Mallorca. The island is owned by Spain and off its coast. Petra is a sunny place filled with flowers, steep cliffs, and ocean breezes.

It is a small town where people live simple lives. No one hurries in Petra. People walk or ride in carts pulled by a horse or mule. Most people then worked as farmers or fishermen. Others worked in stone quarries.

Miguel Jose helped his father farm their small plot of land. He herded sheep and goats. He loved caring for the animals. Their house made of stone was built with a tile roof. This same roof was shared by their animals in a corral next to the kitchen.

He was a small boy for his age and was often sick. The family was afraid for their son. Two children before him had died young. His sister, Juana, was born three years after Miguel. Their family was loving and happy, though poor. Sometimes when the crops did not grow well, Antonio had to cut marble at the quarries.

Religion meant a great deal to the Serra family. Their social lives centered around the church.

Not every child in Petra attended school. But Miguel Jose did and studied hard. He turned to books since he could not play sports like his other classmates. His teachers were impressed by his bright, quick mind.

Finally, the time came when he knew all they could teach him. This was unusual in a town where most of the people could not even read or write. His own parents could not.

A teacher told his parents that he should go to the university in Palma, a nearby town. It was run by the Franciscan priests.

It would mean he could not live with his family anymore. Antonio and Margarita thought long and hard about it. They loved their son very much and knew they would miss him. What future did he have in Petra? Most of the boys became farmers, fishermen, or workers in the quarries. Miguel was not strong enough and too unhealthy for such hard work.

The teacher told them he could get a fine education at Palma. They knew his parents were too poor to send him to a university. This was his chance. With sadness, they decided to let him go. Miguel Jose was fifteen that September of 1729.

SCHOOL AT PALMA

His parents took him to Palma. As he waved goodbye to his sister, a part of him wanted to stay with his family. Another part looked forward to learning new things.

When they reached Palma and the church of St. Francis, Miguel was struck with the beauty of it. His father left him in the care of a priest.

Though he missed his family, Miguel was happy at Palma. His curious mind eagerly learned new subjects. He amazed his teachers.

He admired the priests at the church. He enjoyed reading books about the saints. Best of all was the story of St. Francis, who had been a missionary. Miguel Jose, too, dreamed about traveling to distant lands to teach people about God.

By the time he was sixteen, he was determined to become a priest. But he was short and looked much younger than his age.

He went to Father Perillo and asked permission to become a priest. How could this boy be old enough? The priest thought that he was lying and turned him down.

Miguel Jose turned away sad and upset. This was his dream. His teachers pleaded with Father Perillo. They told him Miguel Jose really was sixteen. Father Perillo changed his mind and let him join.

Miguel Jose put on his long robe and tied the white cord around his waist. He wore sandals on his feet. At last on September 14, 1730, he was accepted to study to become a Franciscan priest.

BECOMING A PRIEST

What was life like for a priest in Spain at that time? He spent six to seven hours a day in prayer. He attended church and ate meals with other priests. Among his duties were studying, teaching, and preaching.

After a year of study, he celebrated being accepted into the priesthood.

He chose a new name. Since he admired St. Francis, he chose the name of his friend, Junipero. Serra decided to pattern his life after the saint. He agreed with him that money and riches were evil. From then on Junipero Serra would live to serve God.

As a priest, he spent many years at the convent of St. Francis. The beginning six years, he studied hard.

The next ten years he became a teacher of philosophy. His classes were always filled. He was popular with his students. The priests at the University of Palma were impressed with Father Junipero Serra. They hoped he would stay at the university forever.

DREAM TO BECOME A MISSIONARY

Serra liked being a teacher.   But he longed to become a missionary. He yearned to teach others about the Christian religion. He especially wanted to teach the Indians who lived faraway and had never heard about it. At the end of 1748, his chance came.

Father Mezquira traveled to Spain to search for priests who wished to become missionaries. Father Mezquira came from the school in Mexico for missionaries. It was called San Fernando College.

Both Father Serra and his good friend and student, Father Palou decided to go. Unfortunately, Father Mezquira had gathered all the missionaries he needed. They only needed people every ten to fifteen years. There was no more room. Would Father Serra ever get to become a missionary? He was already thirty-six years old.

The new missionaries were taken by ship from Palmas to Cadiz, Spain. After this short voyage, some of the priests decided not to become missionaries and dropped out. This left openings for Fathers Serra and Palou. The two were overjoyed.

Father Serra left the island of Mallorca for lands he had never seen. It saddened him to think he would never see his family again.

THE SHIP TO MALAGA

They sailed aboard a ship bound for Malaga, Spain. Other missionaries were waiting for them there. When they arrived, they would all sail to Mexico.

The captain aboard their ship was fearsome. He did not like padres at all. Friends warned them to wait for another ship. There was little time. They did not want to take the chance of being left behind.

On April 13th, 1749, they set sail for Malaga. From the beginning, the captain argued with Father Serra about religion. He defended the Catholic religion and argued back, giving reasons. The captain would not leave Father Serra alone.

Again and again, he pestered Father Serra about religion. The captain had a terrible temper. He grew more angry. He threatened the two padres with a knife. He told them he was going to throw them in the ocean.

The padres thought the captain was crazy. They decided to take turns watching him until the end of the voyage. After two weeks, they were happy to reach Malaga.

Voyage to Mexico

SAILING TO THE NEW WORLD

A friendlier captain aboard a Spanish ship awaited them on their trip to Cadiz, Spain. When they arrived, they discovered their hurrying had been for nothing.

With only nineteen missionaries left, they needed fourteen more. What had happened to the rest of the men? They had changed their minds. Travel by sea at that time was dangerous. Storms battered ships and often sunk them. Some of the priests were afraid to take the long trip. Others decided they would miss their family, friends, and civilization too much.

Finally, more padres joined them on their adventure to the New World. They were divided into two groups. The first of about twenty Franciscan padres were to leave on the ship, *Villasota*. Fathers Serra and Palou sailed aboard.

The voyage lasted ninety-nine days. Can you imagine sailing in a ship without touching land for that long? Food and water ran low. They suffered greatly from thirst.

Serra didn't complain but said, "I have found a means to avoid thirst, to eat little and talk less."

When they reached Puerto Rico, the people warmly welcomed them. They gave them food and water and helped the sick. Eating fresh fruit and vegetables was a treat for the padres. The group rested about two weeks. In return, the padres held church services for the people.

Their new friends helped them stock the ship with food and supplies. They bravely continued their trip.

But soon they found themselves in a terrible storm. The sea tossed and battered their little ship around. This frightened the missionaries.

One of the missionaries suggested they each write down the name of their favorite saint on a slip of paper. They mixed them in a bowl. The name drawn was St. Barbara. "Long live Santa Barbara," they shouted together. The seas did calm down. The ship reached Vera Cruz, Mexico safely.

BY FOOT TO MEXICO CITY

When the ship arrived in Vera Cruz, the padres were tired. Some were sick. Horses and mules were waiting to carry them on the rest of their journey. Swamps around this seaport were overrun with diseases.

Knowing this, Father Serra still wanted to walk the 270 miles to Mexico City. Why? He admired St. Francis, who had always walked everywhere. He wanted to follow his example.

St. Francis never wanted to load down any animal by riding on its back. The distances he traveled were much shorter than those of the missionaries in the New World.

Father Serra and another padre decided to walk. The journey was not easy. They had to cross through blazing deserts, tropical jungles, and rugged mountains. They made friends with strangers who helped them along the way.

It was close to dark one day when they came to a deep stream. The two men didn't know how to cross. While they were talking about it, a man on the other side heard them. He gave them directions and led them safely across.

That night, he invited them to sleep in his house. It was so cold, they would have frozen to death if they had slept outside.

Other people were kind to them. People would give them food to eat. A stranger on horseback gave them fruit. Another man gave them a corn loaf.

Without food or water or a guide, it was not an easy trip. They walked in sandals about fifteen to twenty miles a day.

One night as they slept outside, Father Serra's leg was bitten by an insect. He scratched it in his sleep. When he woke up, it was infected and swollen. They had to rest for several days. The leg was better but it never healed completely. It pained him and caused him to limp for the rest of his life.

The two tired, hungry missionaries arrived at last in Mexico City.

FATHER SERRA IN MEXICO CITY

Father Guardian Velasco warmly greeted them as they arrived at the College of San Fernando. This was the school for missionaries. All mission activities for the New World started here. Mexico City was the headquarters of the Spanish government.

The padres who came to the college promised to stay for at least ten years. Many never went back to Spain.

Father Serra was eager to become a missionary at once. But Father Guardian had other plans for him. New padres served a year at the college to learn how to become a missionary. Father Serra for months preached to the rich people of Mexico City.

He did not like this. He saw how they spent money on unimportant things. He would scold them in church for not sharing their money with the poor. The rich people did not want to hear this.

Father Serra kept dreaming about serving at a mission and teaching the Indians. After five months, his dream came true.

ADVENTURES IN SIERRA GORDA

The Sierra Gorda Missions were north of Mexico City. Padres sent here before did not like it. The climate was so hot and humid. There was so much sickness that many padres had died. The Pame Indians did not seem interested in the Christian religion.

Father Serra was burning with eagerness to go. His friend, Father Palou, traveled with him. They walked for two weeks through swamps and terrible heat until they reached the mission in Jalpan.

When they arrived, they spent many months learning the Indians' language. Serra translated prayers and lessons into Pame. While teaching the Indians about religion, Father Serra realized they were hungry.

He was a practical man. He knew about farming. How better to cure their hunger than to show them how to raise animals and plant crops? They tended pigs and sheep. Their corn, wheat, and other vegetables grew well. No longer did they have to search for all their food on the wild land.

The Mission buildings were not in good shape. Father Serra showed the Indians how to make adobe bricks. They mixed the earth with water and straw. Pouring it into a mold, they left the brick in the sun to dry. They used bricks to repair buildings. He taught them how to work as tanners, carpenters, and blacksmiths.

The women were eager to learn how to weave. They wove fine new clothes and blankets for their people. They traded or sold the extra products.

He tried hard to win the people's trust and hearts. He realized the Indians liked ceremonies. He tried to give them processions, festivals, and plays.

A brave man, he wanted to reach Indians living further in the wilderness. He and Father Palou walked to these villages. It was very dangerous. Poisonous snakes and wild animals roamed the land. Serra believed it was worth risking his life to teach them about God.

He was happy here. He loved the Indians and they loved him. As President of the Sierra Gorda Missions, he was in charge of five. They were Jalpan, Landa, Conca, Tancoyol, and Tilaco. He traveled between them many times during those nine years.

Sierra Gorda Missions & Preaching

UNITED STATES

LOWER CALIFORNIA

MEXICO

Conca . . Tancoyol

Jalpan . . Landa

. Tilaco

. Guadalajara

San Blas .

PACIFIC OCEAN

Morelia . Mexico City

Puebla .

Vera Cruz

Villa Alta .

Oaxaca

WANDERING PREACHER

Suddenly, Fathers Serra and Palou were ordered to return to the College of San Fernando. Father Serra was happy to go wherever he was needed. This time it was to be in Texas at the San Saba Missions. He was overjoyed! He could teach the Apache Indians about Christianity.

But this did not happen. The Indians burned down one of the missions and killed some missionaries. It was not wise to send anymore. The viceroy died and plans were changed.

Serra became a wandering priest. He traveled on the road to rough seaports and mining camps. Sometimes he preached in rich towns. Half the year he traveled. He preached in Guadalajara, Puebla, Oaxaca, and Villa Alta. The rest of the time he lived at the college. He served as a traveling preacher for almost nine years. All this time, he prayed to be assigned to a missionary project.

TAKEOVER OF LOWER CALIFORNIA MISSIONS

Priests of another Catholic religious group called the Jesuits ran the missions of Lower California. (Baja California) King Charles III in Spain became angered by them. He did not give his reasons. In 1767, he told them to leave and return to Spain.

What did this mean to Father Serra and other Franciscan priests? They would have to fill their places.

Soldiers guarded the missions until the new missionaries arrived. But they took many of the goods and animals that belonged to the missions. When the padres arrived, the missions were in poor condition. With zeal, Father Serra started over.

Though he was put in charge of these missions, he stayed only a year. Much of his time was spent planning and preparing for the Upper California expedition.

THE TRAIL TO CALIFORNIA

In 1768 the next plan for Spain was to establish missions in Upper California. Who could better head the missions than Father Junipero Serra? He was chosen President of the missions.

The four expeditions would travel separately. Two ships, the *San Carlos* and the *San Antonio* would bring men and supplies by sea. Two other expeditions would travel by land. They would herd along horses, mules, and animals needed to start the missions.

Much work was involved in preparing for the expeditions. What ships would they take? What people would come? What supplies would be needed?

Sweat dripped from the faces of the men as they loaded up the ships. Father Serra watched them. They hauled dried beef, boxes of chocolate, sacks of corn, wheat, peas, and wine aboard. Axes, hoes, and spades were packed for tilling the soil and planting crops. Church goods such as altars, bells, candles, and priests' robes were needed by the priests.

The ships to sail were in poor condition. The delays for repairs tried Father Serra's patience. At last, the ships sailed out to sea. Next, the two land expeditions were made ready.

Captain Rivera commanded the first by land. With him traveled Father Crespi, twenty-five soldiers, a few muleteers, and forty-two Christian Indians.

Father Serra watched them start off. His eyes were filled with joy at the thought of founding new missions. He was so eager to begin. At last, the order came to start. Don Gaspar de Portola commanded the expedition.

What was it like to travel on an expedition? The day began with Father Serra rising when the sun came up. He held a church service. Meanwhile, the cooks prepared breakfast. Soldiers and Indians saddled the horses and loaded supplies on the backs of the mules.

After breakfast, Portola would cry, "Mount up!" They would be off for another day on the trail.

Portola rode on horseback at the front with Francisco Ortega, sergeant of the soldiers. Twenty soldiers followed in two rows. They were called *leatherjackets* for the buckskin jackets they wore. They wore helmets and carried shields and muskets. Ortega rode ahead to find water and a good campsite.

The cook and his helpers rode behind with mules loaded down with clanking pots and pans. A pack train of over one hundred mules trailed. Food and supplies were lashed to their saddles. Muleteers and some Indians kept watch over them.

A herd of horses came next followed by cattle. The Indian cowboys kept rounding up the strays.

At the end, a dozen leatherjackets rode in the dust, guarding the people.

The expedition was slow. They couldn't travel quickly with all the animals. They needed time to rest and graze. The group traveled only in the morning for four to six miles.

By lunch they stopped. They unsaddled the horses and unloaded the mules. After the meal, they camped for the night.

Father Serra's leg troubled him. It was swollen and painful. He could travel no further. Portola insisted he turn back.

Father Serra would not listen. "Even if I die here on the road, I will not go back," he answered determinedly.

There was no medicine or doctor. Watching a muleteer apply salve to his sick donkey, Serra asked him to heal his leg. The muleteer used the same salve. In several days, Father Serra's leg was much better.

Portola led the party on. Sometimes they traveled through deserts. It could be so hot and dry that they would not find any water. Other times the men and cattle stumbled over steep, rocky paths.

Most of the Indians they visited with on the way were friendly. But some were not.

Several Indians started following them. The soldiers captured one and brought him to Captain Portola. After questioning him, Portola found out other Indians were planning to attack them and steal their cattle.

Portola wanted to send his men to find the Indian braves and kill them. Father Serra pleaded with him. Treat the Indian kindly. Feed him and give him gifts to take to his tribe. Maybe the Indians would change their minds about the attack.

Portola did as Father Serra asked. But he prepared his men for an attack. The Indians returned with gifts and offered their friendship.

Another time, the Christian Indians that had come with them began running away. Father Serra and Commander Portola were puzzled. They wanted to know why. They talked to the other Indians. The Indians were afraid they might be forced to stay in California. Then they would never see their families again. Others said they did not like the way the leatherjackets treated them. Some said one of the cooks did not give them enough to eat.

Portola was angry. The cook was found and punished. Portola made him follow at the end of the expedition on foot. After that, the Indians were happy. No more Indians left.

A group of friendly Indians showed curiosity about the Spaniards. Their clothing and possessions looked strange. They began to touch and explore them.

They liked Father Serra's glasses. He took them off so they could see them close-up. They passed them around then ran off with them. The poor padre knew he could not get another pair out in the wilderness.

With the help of some of the soldiers, he tracked down the Indians. He found his glasses.

After traveling for forty-six days, the party arrived in San Diego on July 1, 1769. In the distance they could see the sails of two ships.

FOUNDING MISSION SAN DIEGO

The ships, the *San Antonio* and the *San Carlos* were anchored in the bay. The men shouted with joy! But as they reached camp, they were shocked by what they saw.

Men were lying sick or dying. Many suffered from the horrible disease called scurvy. It was caused by not eating enough fruit and vegetables on the voyage. The poor men moaned and cried out.

Father Serra knelt down to pray beside a man who was near death.

How had this happened? Father Serra talked to the men. A mistake on their map led them further north.

The *San Antonio* sailed right past San Diego. The voyage stretched longer. By the time they found San Diego, many of the crew were sick or dying.

Men aboard the *San Carlos* battled a storm that almost sunk their ship. The barrels holding their drinking water were leaking. When they stopped to repair the ship, they filled up the barrels with water. It turned out to be bad and made them all sick.

Their camp looked more like a hospital. Healthy people nursed the sick. All around them, men were dying. The expedition seemed like a bad dream.

Portola was sad. He gathered everyone together. He told them that more than half their people had died. He did not know what to do next. Should they give up and return to Mexico? They could try to search again for Monterey.

Why was it so important to reach Monterey? Years ago the explorer, Vizcaino had landed there. In 1602, he had claimed California for Spain. Planting a cross in the ground, he buried important papers under it. They declared that California belonged to Spain.

Russian traders and trappers in Northern California were threatening to take over the land. The Spaniards needed to find Monterey.

Captain Perez took several soldiers and sailors aboard the *San Antonio* to sail to San Blas, Mexico. He picked up food and supplies and a crew of sailors.

Portola led another land expedition to search for Monterey. A group of padres, soldiers, and Christian Indians were left behind. They busily nursed the sick. Men well enough built rough shelters.

On July 16, 1769 Father Serra planted a large wooden cross in the ground. He blessed the cross and rang the bell hanging from a nearby tree. The clanking sounds he hoped would attract the attention of the Indians. He led a church service and named the Mission for a saint. This was the custom when founding each new mission.

The nearby Indians came to visit. Father Serra welcomed their friendship. But there were many troubles with the Indians. They did not like the Spaniards on their land. Several times they attacked the camp.

Another time, the Indians stole from the sick men. They took their sheets off the beds and their shirts from their backs. The leather-jackets shot some of the Indians and wounded others. They came back with their wounded and asked for help. The Spaniards tried to cure them.

At last, Father Serra thought he had won their trust. An Indian couple wanted their baby baptized. At the ceremony, Father Serra was sprinkling holy water on the baby's head. A man grabbed the baby out of his hands and ran off with it. It saddened the padre.

After six months, Portola and his men returned. They were discouraged. They had looked for Monterey Bay, but they did not find it.

Where was the ship, *San Antonio*? Why hadn't it come yet with the needed food and supplies? With all the problems, Portola decided to give up.

Father Serra pleaded with him. The missions would never be founded in Upper California. The Indians would never know God. Secretly, Serra decided he would stay even if everyone else left.

Portola told Serra that if the ship did not come by March 19th (St. Joseph's Day), they would pack up and go back to Mexico. The sails of the *San Antonio* were spotted in the distance that same day. The men shouted and cheered when they saw it.

ESTABLISHING A PRESIDIO AND A MISSION

Portola felt encouraged. After several weeks of rest for the men, he started out again by land. Father Serra sailed aboard the *San Antonio* with another group. This time they found Monterey.

Land for a *presidio* or a fort, and a mission were chosen. On June 3, 1770, Serra planted the wooden cross. He sprinkled it with holy water and blessed it. Soldiers raised the flag of Spain and saluted. Bells rang as soldiers fired their guns in celebration! The new Mission was named San Carlos Borromeo.

Portola traveled by ship and horseback as fast as he could until he reached Mexico City. He announced the good news to the viceroy, Jose de Galvez. Galvez happily told the world.

Monterey became the capital of Upper California. Commander Don Pedro Fages was left in charge. A total of forty soldiers, padres, and Christian Indians were left behind. It was up to them to build the missions and the pueblo. They survived in the wilderness on their own.

Pounding, clanking, and chopping noises rang out as the soldiers cut trees for the new buildings. They built a presidio, a house for him, and one for the padres. Fages worked the men hard, even on Sundays. Father Serra objected.

There were other reasons he was not pleased with Commander Fages. He did not like the way Fages and his soldiers looked down on the Indians. How dare Fages tell him how to run his missions. Neither Serra nor Fages liked to being told what to do.

Frightened by the guns, the Indians did not come the first day. Slowly, they began to make friends with the missionaries. Father Serra was pleased when an Indian couple allowed their son to be baptized. Father Serra was determined to move the Mission away from the fort. He asked the viceroy's permission.

The ship, *San Antonio,* returned with new missionaries and fresh supplies. It also brought bad news. Jose de Galvez was no longer viceroy.

After he fought against the Apache Indians, he went crazy. Serra was worried, though. Galvez was a friend of the missions. Who would take his place?

Viceroy Bucareli sent Father Serra a letter. He read it joyfully. It gave him permission to move the Mission and to found more missions.

Serra moved the Mission to the Carmel Valley. A river flowed through the beautiful land. Trees grew nearby. It overlooked the sparkling blue ocean. Serra made this his headquarters. He lived here when not traveling or founding other missions.

SAN ANTONIO DE PADUA MISSION

Commander Fages was against Father Serra founding another mission. He argued that he couldn't spare the men. Serra pestered him, reminding him of the viceroy's orders. Fages gave in.

Father Serra face's beamed with happiness. Along with Serra traveled Fathers Sitjar and Pieras, a handful of soldiers, sailors, and Christian Indians. By mule, it took them five days to reach the Valley of the Oaks.

On July 14, 1771, Father Serra founded the Mission under a brushwood shelter. Enthusiastically, he rung the bells, calling the

Indians. A young boy appeared. Father Serra gave him a gift of colored glass beads. He held them up to the sunlight and watched them sparkle. Running off, he returned with other Indians. They brought baskets of acorns and pine nuts for the hungry travelers.

A few days later, Father Serra left for Monterey. He hoped to establish Mission San Luis Obispo soon. He could not because there were not enough soldiers.

Building began at once. Within several weeks, the people built a chapel, storehouse, and rooms for the soldiers.

The Indians welcomed them. The Spaniards' troubles came from nature. Too much heat and too little water caused their crops to fail.

The padres decided to move the Mission. The Indians helped them build a water channel. It brought water from the San Miguel Creek to the Mission. Now the wheat crop grew well. Nearby rabbits and squirrels had to be shooed away from nibbling on them.

This Mission made the fastest and best progress. Over one hundred and fifty Indians became Christians in only two years.

SAN GABRIEL DE ARCANGEL MISSION

The expedition was gathering at San Diego Mission. In charge was Corporal Robles. When Commander Fages arrived, he swept him aside. Fages gave the orders now. He yelled at the men and punished them if they did not finish their work. Nine soldiers ran away.

What would they do without these men? They depended on them for the journey. Fages paced back and forth. Finally he talked to Father Paterna. Persuade them to come back, Fages pleaded. He promised not to punish them. But after they returned, he locked them up. He blamed Corporal Robles for their actions. They escaped again, Corporal Robles fleeing with them.

Fages decided not to go on the expedition. Father Serra was stranded in Monterey. Fages had never sent the guard of soldiers to escort Serra. Plans for establishing Missions San Buenaventura and San Luis Obispo had to wait.

Two missionaries, Fathers Cambon and Somera, set out. Only twelve soldiers accompanied them, along with various animals. Fages ordered the soldiers to start building immediately. There would be trouble if they weren't finished by the time he arrived.

As the group approached San Gabriel, a shower of arrows rained down on them. How could they explain to the Indians they wanted to be friends? They didn't speak their language. One of the padres quickly held up a painting of Mary, Mother of Jesus.

A strange thing happened. The Indians stopped fighting. They laid down their weapons and crept closer to the painting. They seemed surprised by its beauty. Running off, they returned to lay food as an offering in front of it.

The padres found a beautiful valley. Two streams watered the land. A forest grew full of oak trees and blackberries. A tribe of friendly Indians lived here. On September 8, 1771, they founded the Mission without Father Serra.

The Indians proved to be quick and eager to help them build. It was lucky because of Fage's orders. He didn't come until October. It took him a long time to round up his runaway soldiers. When he came, he disturbed the friendship developing between the Indians and missionaries. Fearing an attack, he wouldn't allow more than five Indians at the Mission at one time.

Trouble with the soldiers threatened peace at the Mission. They rode into the Indian villages and treated the Indians cruelly. One time they hurt the wife of a chief. Angry, the chief gathered some of his men. They tried to attack the soldier. Instead, one of the soldiers killed the chief.

The Indians visited neighboring tribes and talked to them. Over a hundred Indians gathered and attacked the Mission. All night long the soldiers fought back. Their water, food, and bullets were getting low. Their hopes were running out. In the distance, they spied soldiers from San Diego. The Indians fled.

Father Cambon talked to Fages about what had happened. The killer needed to be punished. The corporal who let the soldiers do these terrible things needed to be punished too. Fages would not listen to him. He did not care what happened to the Indians.

Father Cambon felt defeated. He was afraid the Indians would never come back. More soldiers were assigned to this Mission to protect it.

SAN LUIS OBISPO DE TOLOSA MISSION

Father Serra waited for fourteen months to establish this Mission. He wanted to found it while traveling to San Diego. The way back to Monterey, they wanted to establish the San Buenaventura Mission.

Stopping for a visit at the San Antonio Mission, Father Serra greeted the missionaries. He was pleased by what he saw. Many Christian Indians were living there.

They continued on to San Luis Obispo. It took only a few hours to find a good place in the Valley of the Bears. On September 1, 1772, Serra blessed the fifth mission. This Mission was spaced halfway between Los Angeles and San Francisco. It was named for St. Louis who was of royal blood and had chosen to become a priest.

Father Cavaller was left in charge. Their supplies were low since the other missions were not doing well enough to donate much.

Three months before, the soldiers had come to hunt bear meat for the San Antonio and San Carlos Missions. The people had been starving.

The Indians remembered how they had killed the bears and were grateful to them. Their own bows and arrows were not strong enough to kill the bears. Now Indians brought them deer meat and wild seeds for the Spaniards. The Indians helped them survive.

Many Indians became Christians. Whatever seeds they planted grew into good crops. They paddled out in their canoes in the ocean and caught many different kinds of fish.

A year after its establishment, the Mission was successful in every way.

TROUBLE FOR THE MISSIONS

Serra discovered Fages was making plans to prevent him from founding any new missions. Afraid for their future, Father Serra decided to travel to Mexico to speak to the viceroy. Father Serra was sixty years old and in poor health. He came down with a fever and nearly died on this trip.

Father Serra explained the situation to Bucareli. The viceroy listened carefully. He sided with Father Serra and fired Fages. The new order from Bucareli was to establish more missions. Father Serra smiled with happiness. Returning to Monterey, he began plans to found the San Juan Capistrano Mission.

Eight days after the founding, news came of an Indian attack on the San Diego Mission. The new Mission was abandoned.

Both Capt. Rivera and Col. Don Juan Bautista de Anza arrived with their soldiers in San Diego quickly. They brought peace to the San Diego Mission.

SAN FRANCISCO DE ASIS MISSION

Captain Rivera replaced Fages as commander of the military in Upper California. His personality proved equally difficult to Father Serra.

Founding the San Francisco Mission also needed Capt. Rivera's permission. But he did not want to give it.

Col. Anza's orders from the viceroy were to carry it out. The year before he had picked out the land. He ordered another soldier to lead the expedition.

Lieutenant Moraga led Fathers Francisco Palou and Cambon, his soldiers, and twenty-five families on the trail. They brought with them five hundred cattle and horses. There would be many animals to start this Mission settlement.

Still no word from Rivera. They settled near a lake. For a while, they waited to receive the order. The presidio and the Mission were established without Rivera's permission on June 26, 1776.

Where were the Indians? No curious Indians had come to the founding. Another tribe had scared them off their land. Several months later they returned.

They were not happy to find the Spaniards. They took things from them. The Spaniards fired their noisy guns in the air. The Indians ran off. They were afraid to come around.

This Mission was not a successful mission. There were problems with the weather. The foggy, damp climate was not healthy. Many Indians became sick with white man's diseases and died.

It was difficult to grow crops in the soil. There was much talk about closing this Mission. But it was left open.

SAN JUAN CAPISTRANO MISSION

Ten soldiers set out on the trail with Fathers Lasuen and Amurrio. They reached a beautiful land. The Indians seemed pleasant. On November 1, 1776, the Spaniards founded the Mission.

Only eight days later, news came of an Indian attack at the San Diego Mission. Would they be attacked too? They hurried to the Presidio of San Diego for protection. The San Juan Capistrano Mission would have to wait to be founded.

About six months later, Father Serra sailed aboard the *San Antonio* to San Diego. This trip was to rebuild the San Diego Mission, which was burned down. Captain Choquet, his sailors, and some Christian Indians began to construct new buildings.

Commander Rivera ordered everyone stop their work. He told them about rumors of another Indian attack. He wouldn't try to find out the truth about them.

Father Serra and Captain Choquet were angry. The captain sailed away to report Rivera. Father Serra was afraid the Mission would not be re-established.

Soon twenty-five soldiers rode into San Diego. They carried a letter from Viceroy Bucareli. He asked how the work was going at San Diego and San Juan Capistrano Missions. He asked how the two new missions near San Francisco Bay were doing.

Rivera was worried. What would happen to him if the viceroy found out he had not followed orders? Rivera acted at once. He rode with some of his soldiers to Monterey. He decided to found new missions in the San Francisco Bay area.

Fathers Serra and Amurrio traveled with soldiers to San Juan Capistrano. About a year after its first founding, the Mission was re-established.

The story of this Mission is one of growth. Many Indians wanted to become Christians. The crops grew well. Many herds of cattle roamed the grassy lands. It enjoyed success from its new beginning.

SANTA CLARA DE ASIS MISSION

Commander Rivera led his soldiers and Father Pena to Monterey. When he arrived, he learned that the San Francisco Mission had already been founded.

He traveled with his group to Santa Clara. Discovering a river with many Indian villages around it, he chose the land. On January 12, 1777, Father Pena led the founding ceremony. Named for Saint Claire, it was the first mission named after a woman.

Right away Indians came bearing gifts. They were eager to learn about Christianity. Many of their babies were dying from a disease sweeping through their villages. They brought them to the missionaries to baptize in hope of saving them.

The choice of land proved wise. Clusters of oak trees grew there. The Guadalupe River nearby watered the soil and helped the crops to grow. Christian Indians planted wheat, corn, and vegetables. So much grew that they gave it away to Indians from nearby villages. The Indians gathered acorns and hazelnuts to eat. During the summer, they caught trout in the river.

SAN BUENAVENTURA MISSION

Many problems caused delays in the founding of this Mission. Among them were some of the commanders of Upper California. The Indians in the area were not friendly to the Spaniards. Troubles at other missions made it impossible for the soldiers to be sent here.

Everyone met at the San Gabriel Mission. Father Serra and Governor Felipe de Neve discussed the future of the missions. He had not allowed any missions to be established during his five year of power.

Governor Neve disagreed with Serra. Neve liked the Arizona plan. One missionary was assigned to a mission with only a few soldiers to guard him. Indians did not live at the mission. Many padres had been killed under this plan. Serra did not want it.

Many people came along on this trip to help found the Mission. There was a party of about two hundred fifty people. Soldiers brought their families. Padres and Christian Indians joined them. Besides people, they brought mules, horses, goats, sheep, and cattle.

Why were so many people necessary? They planned to establish the Presidio of Santa Barbara too.

They continued their march, heading for the coast. The site for Mission San Buenaventura was chosen near the beach close to a large town of Indians.

On Easter Day, March 31, 1782, Serra founded this Mission. While Gov. Neve was at the Santa Barbara Presidio site, Serra built the Mission like the others. He ignored the new rule to follow the Arizona plan. It was smoothly running by the time Neve came.

Indians were willing to help build the Mission. They also built a water channel seven miles long to water the grain fields.

When Neve heard how this Mission was built, he delayed the establishment of the Santa Barbara Mission.

THE END OF HIS TRAVELS

Serra realized in 1783, that he was getting old and could not travel much longer. He decided to take a trip and visit all the nine missions one last time.

He sailed from Monterey to San Diego. Then he traveled by mule over the land route. At each mission, he confirmed and baptized everyone who wished it. This trip was too hard on a man as sick as he.

Returning to Carmel, he stayed close to his church and bed. A ship's doctor was brought to him. He tried to help Father Serra but could not. His chest bothered him greatly. It was difficult for him to breathe.

On August 28, 1784, he died at age seventy. He had served as a priest for fifty-three years of his life. He was a missionary for thirty-five years. His friend, Father Palou, gave the ceremony of his funeral.

From all around, people came to say goodbye to Father Serra. He had a great many friends. Indians, soldiers, government leaders, sailors, and other padres.

The church was packed with people. Many had to stand outside during the service. The Indian choir sang. In the afternoon, a parade of people carried his body. Father Palou gave the crowd tiny pieces of cloth cut from Father Serra's clothes. It was a way to remind them of the padre.

His life was a hard one. It was filled with defeat and disappointment. He could have followed the easy life as a teacher in Spain. His heart burned to teach the Indians about Christianity. In his life, he traveled thousands of miles. He did this to teach the Indians about the God he so loved.

As President of the California Missions, he founded nine missions. Others carried on his work after his death. A total of twenty-one missions were established along the coast of California.

Today Father Serra is not forgotten. The missions he built and statues of him serve as reminders. Many people believe he was a hero. The Catholic church is studying about his life. They may soon declare him a saint.

California Missions

San Francisco Solano

San Rafael Arcangel

San Francisco de Asis

San Jose de Guadalupe

Santa Clara de Asis

Santa Cruz

San Juan Bautista

San Carlos Borromeo

Nuestra Senora de la Soledad

San Antonio de Padua

San Miguel Arcangel

San Luis Obispo de Tolosa

La Purisima Concepcion

Santa Ines

San Buenaventura

Santa Barbara

San Fernando Rey de Espana

San Gabriel Arcangel

San Juan Capistrano

San Luis Rey de Francia

San Diego de Alcala

BIBLIOGRAPHY

Ainsworth, Katherine and Edward. *In the Shade of the Juniper Tree: A Life of Fray Junipero Serra*, Doubleday, 1960.

Bolton, Ivy May. *Father Junipero Serra*, Julian Messner, Inc., 1952.

Condon, Vesta. *Father Serra, first great pioneer* in *California*, Harper and Row, 1950.

De Nevi, Don and Noel, Francis Maholy. *Junipero Serra: the Illustrated Story of the Franciscan Founder* of *California's Missions*, Harper, 1985.

Duque, Sally. *California's Father Serra*, Binfords & Mort, 1958.

Englebert, Omer. *The Last of the Conquistadors*, Harcourt, 1956.

Geiger, Maynard. *The Life and Times of Fray Junipero Serra*, Vol. 1-2, Academy of American Franciscan History, 1959.

Geiger, Maynard.(tr) *Palou's Life of Fray Junipero Serra*, Academy of American Franciscan History, 1955.

Habig, Marion. *Man of Greatness*, Franciscan Herald Press, 1963.

Lyngheim, Linda. *The Indians and the California Missions*, Langtry Publications, 1984.

Politi, Leo. *The Mission Bell*, Scribner's, 1953.

Repplier, Agnes. *Junipero Serra, Pioneer Colonist of California*, Doubleday, 1933.

Sullivan, Gertrude Ann. "In His Footsteps, the Life Journey of Father Serra," California Catholic Conference, 1984.

Sullivan, Gertrude Ann. "Rooted in Vision, the Life Journey of Junipero Serra," California Catholic Conference, 1984.

Sullivan, Gertrude Ann. "Small and Mighty, the Story of Junipero Serra," California Catholic Conference, 1984.

Waterhouse, E. *Serra: California Conquistador*, Parker, 1968.

Wise, Winifred. *Fray Junipero Serra and the California Conquest*, Scribner's, 1967.

See also bibliography of The Indians and the California Missions.

INDEX

Adobe bricks 25
Amurrio, Father 52, 53
Animals, raising 8, 21, 24, 29, 32, 51, 53, 57
Anza, Juan Bautista de 49, 50
Bucareli, Antonio Maria 40, 49, 53
Cabrillo, Juan Rodriguez 36
Cadiz, Spain 19
California, Lower 28 Upper 29-57
Cambon, Father 46, 51
Cavaller, Father 48
Charles III, King of Spain 28
Choquet, Capt. 52, 53
Cowboys, Indian 30
Dominican padres 19
Deserts 22
Diseases 21, 35, 36, 51, 55, 58
Expeditions 29, 37, 44
Fages, Don Pedro 39-40, 42, 44, 46, 49
Farming 10, 24, 43, 48, 51, 53, 55
Fishing 10
Franciscan priests 13, 28
Galvez, Jose de 39, 40
Indians 15, 23, 24-25, 27, 30, 33, 34, 37, 40, 43, 45, 47-48, 51-52, 54, 56, 57
Jaime, Father Luis
Jesuit padres 28
Lasuen, Father 52
Mallorca 8
Malaga, Spain 17
Mexico 15, 36
Mezquira, Father 15
Missionaries 15, 27
Missions: Map 60,
    Lower California 28
    San Antonio 42-43, 47
    San Buenaventura 56-57
    San Carlos Borromeo 39-41, 48
    San Diego 35-38, 44, 49, 52, 53
    San Francisco de Asis 50-51, 54
    San Gabriel 44-46
    San Juan Capistrano 49, 52-53
    San Luis Obispo 47-48
    San Saba 27
    Santa Clara 54-55
    Trades 25

Monterey 36, 37, 38, 39, 44, 47, 49, 53, 58
Neve, Felipe de 56-57
New World 19
Ortega, Francisco 30
Palma 10, 12, 14, 15
Palou 15, 17, 24, 25, 27, 51, 58, 59
Paterna, Father 44
Perez, Capt. 37
Petra 8, 10
Pieras, Father 42
Portola, Gaspar de 30, 32, 33, 34, 36, 37
Presidio 39, 40, 52, 57
Priest 12-14, 19-20, 37, 45, 57, 58
Puerto Rico 20
Religion 24, 8, 12
Rivera, Fernando de 30, 49, 50, 51, 53, 54
Robles, Corporal 37
St. Francis 12, 21
San Antonio (ship) 29, 35, 36, 37, 39, 40, 52
San Antonio Mission 42-43, 47
San Buenaventura Mission 45, 47
San Carlos (ship) 29, 35, 36
San Carlos Borremeo Mission 39-41, 48
San Diego Mission 35-38, 52, 53
San Fernando College 23, 27
San Francisco de Asis Mission 50-51, 54
San Gabriel de Arcangel Mission 44-66
San Juan Capistrano Mission 49, 52-53
San Luis Obispo de Tolosa Mission 45, 47-48
San Saba Missions 27
Santa Clara Mission 54-55
Serra, Antonio 6, 10
Serra, Juana 8
Serra, Father Junipero (Miguel Jose) 6, 8-10, 12-14, 15,16, 17, 21-22,
    23, 24-26, 27, 28, 29, 32-33, 40, 42, 49, 56-57, 58, 59
Serra, Margarita 6, 10
Sierra Gorda Missions 24-26, Map 26
Sitjar, Father 42
Soldiers, leatherjackets 28, 30, 32, 34, 37, 40, 44, 45, 46, 52, 53, 54, 57, 58
Spain 39, 59
Villasota (ship) 19
Viceroy 27, 39, 40, 50, 53
Voyages 15, 19, 35-36

ABOUT THE AUTHOR

Linda Lyngheim is a California history enthusiast. She has written other books and pamphlets on California history. *The Indians and the California Missions* is a juvenile book. "The California Rancho Era" and "California Historical Novels" are two pamphlets she has written for adults. She received her Bachelor of Arts degree in social science from Cal State University, Fresno. Her library degree is from University of Southern California. As a librarian, she has worked for the Glendale Public Library. As a past book reviewer for *School Library Journal*, she has also contributed articles to that publication.

ABOUT THE ILLUSTRATOR

Phyllis Garber is a graduate of Carnegie Mellon University. She studied at the Pittsburgh Art Institute and Pasadena School of Art and with Robert Uecker, Patricia Short, Jean Freeman, and David Whelan. She has exhibited in juried shows by the Costa Mesa Art Association. She has received many local art awards for her watercolors.